The Thrush Nest

Written by Catherine Baker

Illustrated by Fabiana Faiallo

Collins

Gran was ill in hospital.

Brent took her a card with a thrush on it.

"There is a thrush nest in my garden – with eggs in!" said Brent.

"Fantastic!" said Gran. "I cannot wait to see!"

Dad had a plan.

7

Dad and Brent put a webcam near the nest.

Then they went back to the hospital.

Dad set up the webcam for Gran on the tablet.

Next morning, Gran rang Brent.

Quick! Look in the nest!

Gran spotted the thrush chicks – from hospital!

Thrush nest

After reading

Letters and Sounds: Phase 4

Word count: 102

Focus on adjacent consonants with short vowel phonemes, e.g. *nest*.

Common exception words: was, there, my, said, to, we, the, they, you, put

Curriculum links: Understanding the world

Curriculum links (National Curriculum, Year 1): Science: Animals, including humans; Computing

Early learning goals: Reading: read and understand simple sentences; use phonic knowledge to decode regular words and read them aloud accurately; read some common irregular words; demonstrate understanding when talking with others about what they have read

National Curriculum learning objectives: Reading/word reading: read accurately by blending sounds in unfamiliar words containing GPCs that have been taught; Reading/comprehension: understand both the books they can already read accurately and fluently and those they listen to by checking that the text makes sense to them as they read, and correcting inaccurate reading

Developing fluency

- Encourage your child to follow the words as you read the first pages with expression, adding emphasis to sentences with exclamation marks.
- Take turns to read a page, encouraging your child to pause at commas and the dashes on pages 4 and 13.

Phonic practice

- Practise reading words that contain adjacent consonants. Encourage your child to sound out and blend the following:

  plan   nest   thrush   went
- Challenge your child to sound out these longer words, breaking them down into syllables to help them.

  gar/den   hos/pi/tal   spott/ed   web/cam   fan/tas/tic

Extending vocabulary

- Challenge your child to think of words that have a similar meaning to these.

  ill (e.g. *poorly, unwell*)   fantastic (e.g. *great, wonderful*)   spotted (e.g. *noticed, saw*)
- Support your child in using a dictionary or thesaurus to find more words with a similar meaning, too.